Ouachita Girl

(Volume 1)

By

Linda Rae Johnson

ISBN: 1-4033-1962-6 (E-book)
ISBN: 1-4033-1963-4 (Paperback)

This book is printed on acid free paper.

1stBooks - rev. 09/04/02

"When we are young, what happens is not nearly as important as what we think happens. Perhaps that's true even when we are not so young."

From Roger Ebert's 1995 review of the film "Hope and Glory"

COMMENTS FROM
LINDA RAE'S AUDIENCE

"Linda Rae is a delightful writer and storyteller. Through her 'creative memoir' genre, she is at once entertaining and vulnerable, as she invites her audience into the most hilarious and personal of all spaces - her childhood."

"Attending a reading performance by Linda Rae is a trip back into childhood and life memories that brings you laughter, tears, and insight. Knowing more about who I am and how I got there was never as much fun as when I experienced this through Linda Rae's performance, a tremendous family drama of life, love, and laughter!"

"Linda Rae has a unique way of sizing up her Louisiana childhood with an entertaining and zany bend. Although some of the memories allow you to see that her past was not always the ideal, her humor completely offsets any of the dreariness you might expect. I laugh heartily at the way she nails her characters and 'the way it is' in good old Dixieland.

"A warm spirit, humor, nostalgia, and insightful characterizations of real people are offered by Linda Rae in her monologues; her performances are a deep, dramatic source of bittersweet pleasure and feminine philosophy."

"There is something so engaging about that which is truly genuine. Linda Rae's words and performances embody just that. There is an innocence and a clarity to her work that simply will not let you go."

"Linda Rae tells it like it was! Her stories take me right back to my childhood growing up in the rural South. She had the audience weeping with laughter."

"Linda writes and reads stories from her experiences that are pitch perfect in capturing the time and place of the South through the eyes of her childhood. Some are poignant, some outright hilarious. She is a gentle, but sharp observer of the human condition and of her kooky family dynamics."

This book is dedicated with grateful love to the
sweet inspirations,
Mama and my three sisters,
Phyllis Freeman
Cathy Hall
Janice Galyen
Sharon Saloutos
And to the memory of our father
for bringing us home again
Raymond (Peanut) Hunt
1924-2000

Table of Contents

Introduction.. xiii

Monopoly at Twelve 1

Dickie Madearis Threw It At Me 4

West Monroe, Louisiana 9

Go Fish... 15

Broomfield's 20

Bowling Alley Wax 25

Playing Among the Dead... 28

Port Arthur or Bust... 34

The Wheelchair.. 40

Observing Arilla.. 47

Two Dimwit Cousins... 53

Loathing Lettie.. 60

Uncovering Santa.. 67

Rosemary and Theodore 73

Not Far From Dallas... 77

Going Home with Peanut 85

Introduction

In July of 1997 at a family get-together, my three sisters and I got into a lively, heated and humorous discussion about our childhood in Louisiana. We laughed about the craziness of it all, recalling incidences that had buried themselves in the subconscious of our minds. During that evening of discussion, we came back to the one argument that had been going on for years. "Who really cheated at Monopoly?"

There we were, grown women in our forties still defending our innocence and as always, trying to pull Mama into it, appealing to her to be the arbitrator. She has refused in our adult lives to play that role.

That evening I returned home and wrote "Monopoly at Twelve," the beginning of "Ouachita Girl." From the first word, I became Linda Rae again and knew I had discovered a voice within myself that had something to say. As I slowly embarked on recreating those days in Louisiana filled with humor, spirit and dark tones of what I refer to as "Southern Discomfort" the voice became a part of me. In the editing process, as I read and re-read each story aloud, I realized I had reconnected to that child within myself.

The reading aloud of these stories developed into a wonderful outlet for me of becoming a performance reader and I have transformed myself into "little Linda Rae" in front of over seventy-five audiences and still counting. I have these first eleven stories on CDs but have decided now is the time to see them in print. I want the words and the "voice" of Linda Rae to ring as strong as the spoken word.

My hope is that as you read these stories, Linda Rae will touch that child within you, recalling some of your own childhood memories with fondness. I celebrate the child within us all because it gives us hope, belief in ourselves and keeps us forever young.

Linda Johnson
Richmond, VA.
March 12, 2002

Monopoly at Twelve

It is too hot for me and my sister, Cathy Lee, to do anything else but play Monopoly. We sprawl across the bare living room floor where it does seem a few degrees cooler than the rest of the house. Mama stomps in from the kitchen, swinging a spatula yelling, "Ya'll get on outside, right now, cause that fussing over which one is cheating is getting on my damn nerves."

I do not cheat, but I always keep one eye on Cathy Lee - two sharp eyes if she is the banker and makes too much change for herself. She is the meanest person I know and even though I am eighteen months older and twenty pounds heavier, she can beat me up and that unnerves me badly. I am a lot smarter than Cathy Lee and she hates that. She is stupid. Cathy Lee has to own Baltic and Mediterranean, which are truly the skid rows of all the avenues, just because her favorite color is purple. It gets her nowhere and is the reason I always win.

I am laughing and howling when Cathy Lee lands on Park Place with my hotel sitting there, rent $1,500 and no chance of making it past Go for that piddly $200. I use my brilliant book brain to carefully select the words that will drive her into a rage, reminding her as I hold my nose, "Don't get mad, Stinky! You still got B.O. Railroad." She despises that joke and as she picks up the board and hurls it across the room, informs me "NOW, Miss Shit, the game is over!" Her silver racing car and my little top hat slam against the wall. The orange and yellow cards are all mixed up, but look pretty on the faded floor.

"Mama, Cathy Lee said the bad word that starts with SH and ends with IT!" Fearing a mouth washing with a bar of Ivory, Cathy Lee jumps up and storms through the screen door hard enough to pull the hinge loose and now the door is hanging crooked. I'll have to spend time on my belly reaching under the sofa to retrieve the deeds and colored money. Then I'll have to find and count all the red hotels and little green houses. The part that will take the longest is getting all the pieces and the money lined up and stacked neatly in them little cardboard compartments. I don't mind, though, cause I love playing Monopoly.

Dickie Madearis Threw It At Me

I'm no sissy and I ain't afraid of snakes, well at least not ones that have been dead for a long time or live ones hanging in trees far away. One thing Louisiana has plenty of and that's snakes. They can sometimes be real mean and chase you and if you get bit by one, believe me, it's all over. You gotta go to the hospital, get shots in your belly and most times even that don't work. You're lucky if the doctor just cuts off the part of you near the snakebite to get all that poison out, but even then you are most likely to swell up and die. I know this is the truth, cause Dickie Madearis told me and his uncle works in the laundry room at St. Francis Hospital.

I love Dickie Madearis. He's the cutest boy in the whole fourth grade. His family moved here from Galveston, Texas and that's real close to the Gulf of Mexico. Dickie must've done a lot of

4

swimming in the gulf cause he's got this beautiful tanned skin and real white teeth. Mr. Madearis drives a truck for Piggly-Wiggly and likes to cook hot and spicy foods. Dickie's mama is a beauty operator and has her own shop, Margie's House of Style, which has four sinks and six hair dryers. Mama gets her hair done there every Tuesday morning cause she says, "There is no one in West Monroe who can pincurl and set a good hairdo like Margie Madearis."

Friday was the last day of school and I was feeling happy walking home even though I was loaded down with my cigar box and all the papers that I'd cleaned out of my desk. Dickie and three other boys from our class was a little ways behind me so I started walking real slow hoping they'd catch up with me. Dickie didn't pay me one bit of attention as they raced past me laughing and trying to trip each other up like fourth grade boys do. I saw em slow down up ahead, gathering round in the middle of the road, looking down at something. I thought it must've been a little baby turtle who'd lost its mama or a frog with a broken leg that Dickie would probably help save.

I saw Dickie run over to the ditch, pull out a long stick and then hurry back over to the road. I was getting closer to them now, and just when I got to where they was, Dickie turned around and there on the end of that stick was a big ol' snake. It looked dead, all smushed in the middle like a huge truck had run over it, but it still scared me and I was screaming plenty loud as I ran past him. Dickie started chasing me with that snake and yelling, "Look out, Linda Rae. It's a water moccasin and it's gonna bite ya."

Dickie then heaved that snake at me which hit me right on my back and that snake's head went partways down the back of my new yellow sundress. I dropped my cigar box, crayons rolling across every part of the road and my papers flying everywhere. I didn't stop running or screaming 'til

I got to my front yard. By that time, the snake had fallen out of my dress, but I could still hear Dickie and them boys laughing at me.

Mama heard me screaming and came running out in the front yard to see what was going on. All I could do was cry out, "Mama, Dickie Madearis threw a snake at me." She ran down the road hollering at them, but when they saw how mad she was, they took off in four different directions. Mama came back, ran into the house slamming the screen door, yelling, "That little hellion, I'm gonna call Margie right now, and believe me, he's gonna get it."

I didn't want Dickie to get it, but that's exactly what happened. He had to clean up all my school stuff from the road and bring it to my house and apologize to me and Mama. I heard he got a whipping that night when his daddy got home from the Piggly-Wiggly. This past week when the ice cream truck came by, Dickie had to sit in his carport and watch all us kids from Jersey Avenue standing around eating push-ups and nutty buddies.

I am not a big mouth tattletale like my sister, Cathy Lee, calls me. I hope Dickie can at least go with his family this summer to visit his grandma in Galveston and go swimming in the Gulf. And I hope by the time fifth grade starts, he will speak to me again. I still do love Dickie Madearis, but he ought not've thrown that snake at me.

West Monroe, Louisiana

The place where I live and come from right now is West Monroe, Louisiana which you shouldn't get mixed up with Monroe. There is a lot that divides these two places and I'm not just talking about the Ouachita River. I love saying that name, Ouachita, and hearing the way it sounds. Mama says the Ouachita is named after a famous Indian chief, which means he probably grew up in Monroe. On their side of the river are cute little wooden boats and lots of fishing piers and multi-colored snow cones for sale. On our side is an ol' cottonseed mill, but it has a wonderful smell, almost like bacon frying. It is where cottonseed oil is made, but I don't know what that's used for.

People who live in Monroe hardly ever come over to West Monroe. They're like a city and we're more like a little town. There are some people from Monroe buried in Pinehurst Cemetery which is just across Arkansas Road from where I live, but I don't think they count cause they're dead.

If me and my sisters wanna get root beer in frosted mugs, then Mama has to drive us across the bridge to the Frost Top. We don't have a bowling alley in West Monroe so we have to go over there to Southern Bowl. In the summer, if we wanna go swimming, the only public pool or picnic table is in Monroe. Johnny Cash even went there to sing at Neville High School last year. Too bad he didn't get over here to West Monroe cause I think he would've liked it a lot.

Along the Ouachita in Monroe you can drive for blocks on Desaird Avenue and see long lines of big magnolia trees, on both sides, making a shady tunnel to drive through. I love to hang out the car window and smell the magnolias but Mama always yells at me, "Linda Rae, get your witless head back in this car, right now." There are pretty houses along Desaird hidden behind the trees, even one house that looks like a mansion, with a glass porch on its side where there are tiny little birds, all beautiful colors, flying around.

On the Ouachita in West Monroe, we don't have many magnolia trees or big houses, just a levee wall that has lots of cracks with weeds growing out of em. The Neville Rebels don't even play the West Monroe High School Colonels cause we've never been good enough, but that's cause our football field looks like a big cereal bowl and always has five inches of muddy water in it. In Monroe, there is Northeast Louisiana State College. We don't have a college in West Monroe, in fact I'm pretty sure there's no one who lives here that's ever been to college.

What we do have is a lot of great places, like Grantham's Furniture Store, which my friend, Lettie Grantham's daddy owns. Me and Lettie love running wild in that store, with twelve rooms of furniture to hide behind and jump on, especially if

Mr. Grantham is on the phone back in his office. Playing house there is fun, too, a lot better than lining up pine needles in your back yard and piling up old cardboard boxes to look like furniture.

We also have a movie theater in West Monroe, the Rialto, which has double features on Saturday afternoons. We get to see the newest Elvis movies, but only after Monroe is finished with em'. Walt's Restaurant which is hooked onto Walt's Motel has the best food anywhere in West Monroe. I even heard that some of the people lined up outside of Walt's on Friday nights waiting to eat his T-bone steaks are from Monroe.

West Monroe does have a little private swimming pool with a snack bar and a nine-hole golf course nearby. The animal shelter is right behind the golf course, so sometimes the golfers can hear dogs yelping. Once in a while, I get to go with Lettie to the swimming pool and she can order us club sandwiches and just charge it on her daddy's bill. Its almost as if the Granthams belong in Monroe.

We don't have a Piggly-Wiggly in West Monroe but we do have Hogans. I love the sign over the front ·door painted like a rainbow which says "Hustle to Hogans." There's a big trailer park behind Hogans, but I only know one kid from my fourth grade class that lives there, Dinky Schoonover. Mostly its just old people or really poor families whose daddies are out of work, drunks, or in jail. You can't hang anything on the walls in them trailers and the bedrooms only have room for half a bed and a little teeny dresser to put all your clothes in. Mama says Monroe don't even have a trailer park.

One thing West Monroe does have is a lot of churches, almost one on every other block cause if there's one thing people here believe in, that's going to church every Sunday morning and sometimes after supper on Sunday evenings.

West Monroe don't have a lot of stop lights so you can ride your bike anywhere, even downtown. You could never ride your bike in Monroe, you'd get hit by a car for sure, 'cause the people there drive way too fast. I guess they're always in a hurry to get to Southern Bowl, the Frost Top or the Piggly-Wiggly.

Go Fish

I always feel lucky on those lazy, muggy summer afternoons when Bill takes me and my sisters, Cathy Lee and Jannie Mae, fishing to Bayou Menareau. It is a nice break for Mama, too, who gets to enjoy the calm of several hours away from Bill and his ranting and raving. After she puts my little sister, Sharon Rose, down for a nap, Mama paints her nails while she gossips on the phone with Mrs. Demoss. Later she sprawls across her bed and reads *True Romance*. My Sunday school teacher, Miss Caroline Breeden, says that those sinful magazines are the downfall of many young women. I don't think she's talking about Mama, though, cause Mama's almost thirty-two and already had her downfall when she hooked up with Bill.

I don't like painted nails or *True Romance* but I do love fishing. I'm only ten and a half but I can bait my own hook with the biggest worm in Bill's bucket. You gotta skewer the worm two or three times to hide the hook real good, which Bill says will usually fool a dumb fish. Since I am the oldest and therefore the bravest of my sisters, I always bait Cathy Lee's and Jannie Mae's hooks, as they cannot stand to pick up or even touch a live worm.

We don't have fancy fly rods like the one Bill has, but we do have sturdy cane poles with clear plastic lines and them little red and white balls that bob up and down on the water. We always try to fly fish the way Bill does, but his temper, which usually gets its way, makes him yell, "Dammit all, quit heaving those poles over your head, cause the next one that gets their hook caught in a tree is gonna get their ass whipped." Bill is my stepfather and sometimes he can be real mean.

There is a big difference in fishing and catching a fish. Bill says fishing is just standing still and keeping your big mouth shut and watching the line, the water and the little plastic bobber. But you gotta know just when to snap back on your pole real hard the second that bobber disappears under the water. You have fooled another stupid fish and can't help but squeal and holler while you are fightin real hard to pull him in. That is called catching a fish and I'm real good at that.

It's always hard for us to keep our big mouths shut, especially when we have to pee. Bill goes crazy if he has to stop fishing and show us the way down to the honeysuckle bushes. He hates standing guard and he always yells at me, "Hurry up, Linda Rae, we ain't got all damn day" which means sometimes I end up peeing on my red tennis shoes.

About four o'clock we pile in the car with all our fish and head back home. Me and my sisters sing songs real quiet in the back seat, so as not to disturb Bill, always ending up with my favorite, *Found a Peanut.*

I'm real good at gutting and cleaning fish. Sometimes the gutting part makes me feel like I'm gonna throw up, but I haven't yet. My favorite part is scraping the scales off with a spoon. Bill always cuts the fish heads off cause I don't know how to do that. Me and Jannie Mae like to take the end of the spoon and poke out the fish eyes.

After there are no eyeballs left in the fish heads to stare back at us, we wrap up the guts in newspaper and throw them in our trash can out in the alley. We have to put the lid on real tight so all the cats from Jersey Avenue won't go crazy during the night trying to get at them smelly fish parts. After that, it's fun rinsing the fish under the hose in our backyard cause we always end up getting our clothes soaking wet. Mama yells at us from the kitchen window, "Ya'll quit turning the hose on your little sister and knocking her down." But Sharon Rose don't seem to mind. She always laughs when she hits the ground.

Around five o'clock, Mama starts getting ready for our fish fry supper. She lets me help beat the eggs and fill the brown paper bag with corn meal. She uses her big black iron skillet to fry the fish in. I love Mama's coleslaw with lots of mayonnaise and pickles, but especially her french fried potatoes.

After a day at Bayou Menareau I am content, my belly filled up with fried fish, and my face all warm from the day's sun. I am so sleepy my eyes won't hardly stay open. Bill even seems content after a good fish day and I like to lay in bed and listen to him and Mama out on the carport, talking low and rocking gently back and forth in the glider, sharing a glass of iced tea and their last cigarette of the evening. I am smiling as I fall asleep, thinking about the next time when me and Cathy Lee and Jannie Mae can go fish, even if it is with Bill.

Broomfield's

It's 5 minutes to 3. I'm sitting at my desk holding my quarter from the tooth fairy so tight, my hand is sweatin'. I keep sneakin' a look at the clock and just waiting for the bell to ring. I'm trying to fool Mrs. Walden by pretending to work the crossword puzzle in my Weekly Reader. And I'm thinking no matter how ugly my grin is, I am the luckiest kid in the whole third grade. I'm only a few minutes and one block away from spending that whole twenty-five cents at Broomfield's.

Broomfield's Store is the best place in the world to spend money. It's full of candy, ice cream, funny books, Coca-Colas and great toys. They even have things for grown ups, like Lucky Strikes, Chase & Sanborn coffee, kitchen matches and cast iron frying pans. Mr. Broomfield sells a lot of car oil. He keeps cases of it stacked in front of the candy counter. That's for the little kids like my sister,

Sharon Rose to stand on, so they can see into the glass case filled with penny candy and Bazooka bubble gum. Sometimes when it's hot the store smells like car oil and you can taste a little bit of that oil in the bubble gum.

Mr. Broomfield's a short, fat guy with a big bald head. He always wears a huge white apron, I guess to hide his big belly. He spends a lot of time sweeping the floor and putting up stock while he's listening to hillbilly music on his transistor radio. He has a fat daughter, Luanne who works there every day after she gets out of high school. It's a wonder Mr. Broomfield can keep anything on them shelves cause every time you go in there, Luanne is always eatin'. She sits on the stool behind the candy counter, with her fat butt hanging off the edge, slurping on a push-up or hogging down a bag of potato chips. Luanne is supposed to keep an eye on the kids in there to make sure nothing gets stolen. When we're walking down the aisles looking at stuff, she leans way over to the side spying on us, cause she is too fat and lazy to get off that stool.

Mr. Broomfield has three rules that you must obey or you will get kicked out sure as shootin'. No.1 - No eatin' or drinkin' in the store. No.2 - No readin' funny books without paying for em first. And No.3 - No loafin'. It get's crowded in there after school and Mr. Broomfield yells at the loafers, "Hey, this ain't a filling station, if you're not buying, then there's the door."

Broomfield 's has lots of great toys, like yo-yos, paddle balls, cap guns and little magnifying glasses which we use to burn up ants on the sidewalk. They was the first store in town to get hoola hoops, black ones at first, then all different colors with the beads inside that makes that shoop-shoop noise when you really get em going. Mr. Broomfield keeps the hoola-hoops hanging on big nails over the candy counter.

At Broomfield's, the hardest thing is to figure out is what you wanna buy especially if you only got a dime. My favorite is a Sugar Daddy sucker but it makes my mouth sore after my teeth have wrestled it for about an hour. Sometimes me and my sister, Cathy Lee go in together and buy a box of L&M candy cigarettes. On the way home we pretend we're smoking and blowing smoke rings just like Bill. I love eatin' the little boxes of salty pretzel sticks wrapped in cellophane and then chugging a Coca-cola afterwards. Its fun looking on the bottom of the bottle to see the name of the city where the Coca-Cola was bottled. If you get one with a far-away city, you get to make a big wish.

My rich friend Lettie Grantham who gets $3 a week allowance for doing nothing always carries lots of nickel and dimes in her red plastic pocketbook. She can have her pick of anything at Broomfield's. One time I saw her spend 82 cents. She bought a Big Time and a Zagnut candy bar, a Grape Ne-Hi, a Mighty Mouse coloring book, a candy necklace, three fireballs, and a little metal tea set and it won't even her birthday.

In the summer Mama is always sending us to Broomfield's mostly to get a loaf of Sunbeam bread, sliced bologna, Duz detergent and the newest *True Romance*. Sometimes on Saturdays, Mama gives me a dollar and says, "Linda Rae, run on down to Broomfields and get a bottle of Prell and two packs of bobby pins so I can do yall's hair tonight for Sunday School."

When I grow up and get married, I hope I'll have lots of pretty dresses, three baby boys, and a husband who owns a store just like Broomfields. What a wonderful life, gettin rich filling up the cash register every day, eating all the Fritoes and Nutty Buddys I want, listening to the radio and reading every Archie funny book in the store.

Bowling Alley Wax

I hate it when Mama bangs on our bedroom door so early. It seems the night has barely said good-morning to the sun. I know that just across Arkansas Road, my best friend, Billie Stell, and her little sister, Hankie, are still sleeping. Their mama is frying bacon and stirring grits, humming softly so as not to wake them.

I hear the vacuum cleaner out in our hallway, scraping against the tired floor and I know that my Mama is not humming. She comes busting through the door, yelling "Ya'll get up, rise and shine! Get on out in the kitchen and fix you a bowl of cereal. We gotta clean this filthy, dirty house. Come on, now!" Me and my sisters don't ever think the house looks dirty, but every Saturday morning it's the same old thing and there ain't no way of getting out of it.

Mama's pulled out all the cleaning supplies from the pantry, spray bottles, jars and cans, each with their own separate stink. There are rags everywhere - long time ago used to be our white cotton underwear. There are greasy, oily rags to shine the furniture. There are wet ones, some loaded with pine oil for the walls and woodwork, and some with bleach for tackling the commode. Then there are the rags reeking with ammonia for cleaning every window, mirror and piece of glass in the house.

The biggest rag of all, Mama's white cotton underwear with the elastic all busted out, is stuffed down into a can of Johnson's bowling alley wax. It's the job I hate the most, as there are five rooms of hardwood floors in our house. Later in the afternoon, while I'm on my hands and knees, making shiny circles on the living room floor, I think about Billie Stell. Her mama will be dropping her and Hankie off at Southern Bowl in their new green Nash Rambler. She will give them a dollar each for bowling, milk duds and a cherry smash. While my sisters and I are emptying out every drawer on our beds so we can match socks and fold nightgowns into neat piles, Billie will be flirting with KK Miller, champion of the pinballs at Southern Bowl.

Billie will stop by later around four and ask if I wanna go bike riding and I'll tell her we ain't finished cleaning yet, to come on back after supper. Later, while wiping down the window sills in the living room, I catch a glimpse of her daddy at their brick barbecue pit that he built all by himself, turning hot dogs and smoking a Lucky and I am wondering why life seems so unfair, especially on Saturdays.

Playing Among the Dead

There's not a whole lot of places for me and my sisters to play in West Monroe. Course we got the playground at school, but who wants to spend time in a place when you already gotta play there five days a week? We used to have softball games over in Billie Stell's backyard until Downey McLemore hit a homer and cracked the windshield on Mr. Stell's new Nash Rambler. After we get one of those big Louisiana downpours, we can sometimes talk Mama into letting us put on our bathing suits and go swimming in the ditch out in front of our house. We get tired of that after a while, it's too shallow to dive, it kinda stinks, plus the crawfish start biting our toes.

It used to be fun to walk down to Mr. Boudreaux's pond and feed his geese, but when we'd run out of stale bread, they'd get this mean look, start honking real loud and chasing us. Then we'd end up in his orchard picking and eating green apples, till one afternoon last summer, Mr. Boudreaux saw us and called Mama and warned her he better not ever see us on his property again. That was the end of all that fun.

We did find a wonderful place to play for a while, which Mama never knew about, and that was Pinehurst Cemetery just across Arkansas Road. It's got lots of rolling hills scattered with tall pines, live oaks and big cypress with limbs full of Spanish moss. It was a perfect place for climbing. We loved playing hide and seek there, too, cause with all them trees and gravestones and statues, you could hide for a real long time before anybody found ya.

Another game me and my sisters loved playing in Pinehurst was counting out loud to fifty to see who could pick the most locust shells off the trees. Mrs. Ballard, my fifth grade teacher, says the locust, which kinda looks like a fat grasshopper, finds a tree to hang onto and then climbs out of its shell leaving it behind, looking like a thick, brown onion skin. I don't mind their shells but I am scared to death of live locusts cause you remember what they did back in the Bible days and, believe me, it wouldn't take too many of em to wipe out West Monroe.

In the winter, we don't hardly ever get snow, and even if we do it's only the powdered sugar kind, which you can't even make a decent snowball out of. But back in January a big ice storm hit town and everything was frozen solid and looked all sparkling like Mama's rhinestone bracelets. We went up to Hogans and found some big cardboard boxes behind the store which we flattened out and went sliding down them hills in Pinehurst and I'm not kidding, we was going fifty miles an hour. Jannie Mae lost control of her box and hit a gravestone, which busted her lip real bad, but I told Mama that she fell down playing tag on Jersey Avenue.

Way in the back of the cemetery is a big statue of Mary, about as tall as a house, with her arms stretched out to the sides, I guess to protect all the dead Catholics buried there. Cathy Lee once dared Downey to climb to the top of that statue. He made it up about as high as her shoulders, when this old man who was driving thru the cemetery, started yelling at us, "You damn kids get away from there and out of here right now before I call the police." It really scared us, especially Downey who hit the ground so hard when he jumped, he busted his knee. We took off...but two days later, we was back over there.

Now, Pinehurst Cemetery was not all games and fun times. There was a lot of sad people who went there, especially one lady we met, Mrs. Lilah Hamrick. She would visit there every Saturday around 4 o'clock. We'd always talk to her and she never seemed to mind that we was playing in the cemetery. Her little girl, Rosalyn, was buried there, not under the ground, but in a big pink marble box with angels and flowers carved all over it. Rosalyn died eight months ago and was only four years old. There's a round picture of her under glass on the front of that pink box with words carved beneath it that say "Tread softly for an angel lies here." Course, you know big mouth Cathy Lee had to ask Mrs. Hamrick how her little girl died, which I thought was real rude but that's Cathy Lee for ya, no respect for the dead and not much for the living. Mrs. Hamrick told us little Rosalyn was born with a big hole in her heart, couldn't run or play and finally got so sick, God took her to be with Him in heaven.

Every evening we had to get out of the cemetery by sunset cause that's when the caretaker, Mr. Shelton, closed and locked the two front gates. Well he calls himself the caretaker, but who's he taking care of? Everybody over there's dead. He is hateful and chased us outta there twice, once when we was playing tag, but he couldn't catch us cause he's got a gimpy leg, plus the fact we can run real fast. The second time he chased us last Saturday, I heard him yelling out our last name which scared me as there is only one Fordyce in the phone book and that's us.

I don't even wanna think about what Mama would do if she found out we'd been playing in Pinehurst Cemetery. I guess now we gotta find a new place to play. Mary Louise Jeter came by this morning and invited us over to see her new dollhouse that she got for her birthday. Cathy Lee and Jannie Mae got all excited and took off. Not me, I think I'd rather wait for another downpour, go swimming in the ditch and let the crawfish bite my toes.

Linda Rae Johnson

Port Arthur or Bust

I dread going back to school next month and hearing kids in my fifth grade class talking about their summer vacations. Traveling in roomy station wagons or by train to fun and far-a-way places like Pine Bluff, Arkansas, Biloxi, Mississippi and Macon, Georgia. Camping in the cool Tennessee mountains or swimming at beaches along the Gulf, bringing home paper bags full of shells and wearing colorful souvenir T-shirts.

And where did we get to spend another summer vacation for a week in July? In the ugly, smelly town of Port Arthur, Texas. There's not one exciting thing to do there which is why they don't have a souvenir T-shirt. Port Arthur is filled with rusted out cars sittin in front of crummy little houses with busted out windows. Alleys with skinny cats and dogs snackin out of garbage cans. And the swimming holes? Scum and mosquitoes on the top

34

and broken beer bottles on the bottom. But the worse thing about Port Arthur is the oil refineries. They're everywhere and make the air hot and yellow with a stink like rotten eggs and black-eyed peas mashed together. Port Arthur is also the place where my stepfather, Bill, was born and grew up, which explains the reason he turned out like he did.

It took seven hours to get to Port Arthur, seven long hours for me and my sisters cooped up in the back seat of the Studebaker with no air-conditioning. Mama packed a bag full of sandwiches, bologna and peanut butter and jelly, a jug of lemonade for us and a thermos of coffee for Bill. After we loaded up the car, Bill informed us, "All right, whoever has to pee better do it now, cause once we pull out of here, we're not stopping." I think the hardest thing in the world is trying to force yourself to pee when you just don't have to. Mama tried to help by turning on the water in the bathroom sink, but that never works, so we had to take along two big mason jars. Believe me, it was no fun squatting on the floor of the car peeing in a jar with Cathy Lee's big feet stuck in my back while Bill was speeding along curvy roads going 50 miles an hour. We didn't have to wipe.

The trip to Port Arthur was more boring than sitting thru church. We took coloring books but with the way Bill drives it's hard to stay inside the lines or connect the dots. Outside of Bunkie Mama sweet talked Bill into turning on the radio and we sang along real soft with Connie Frances, the Everly Brothers and Fats Domino. My sisters brought along funny books to read, but that always makes me car sick. And it didn't help none with hot air blowing in the windows and Bill and Mama smoking L&Ms the whole way. I had to fight that sick feeling in my stomach cause you know if Bill wouldn't stop to let us pee, he sure wandn't gonna stop for me to throw up. He did let me climb up in the front seat and sit next to Mama and hang my head out the window which helped a little.

The reason Bill was in such a big hurry to get to Port Arthur was to see his Mama, Ida. Bill's daddy is dead. He worked in one of them refineries and choked to death on that hot, yellow air.

Ida is a real ugly woman with eyes that look like they're about ready to pop out of her head. She has a teeny little hole for a mouth and her hair looks dried out like steel wool and is the color of navy bean soup. Mama, whose hair always looks so perfect, says "That old woman don't even know what a comb or brush is." Ida's skin is gray and whenever I get up real close to her, she looks like she just about two hours away from dead. She wears ugly black clunky shoes laced up tight enough to choke her skinny legs. Ida moves like an old turtle so it takes forever for her to do anything, including fixing our breakfast, which she calls a bowl of cream of wheat and half a banana. We were lucky if we go fed by 10 o'clock. Mama offered to help her in the kitchen but that nasty old hag hollered at her, "No, Phyllis, this is my kitchen and I'll do the cookin. Just get on outta here." Ida is another reason Bill turned out like he did.

Ida lives in a teeny-tiny house way too small for the six of us to sleep in. Bill call's it cozy. I call Bill cheap. That tightwad would never let us stay in a motel, especially one with a swimming pool. So me and my sisters had to sleep on a mattress on Ida's living room floor. There's a huge painting of her brother, Lester who got killed in World War I, hanging on the living room wall. He's got these big creepy eyes that are always staring down at you or following you to the bathroom in the middle of the night.

Sunday. was my favorite day in Port Arthur. That's cause we packed up the car, rinsed out the mason jars and got ready to head back home. Ida made us egg salad sandwiches and her lousy homemade dill pickles. Bill even makes a face when he eats em.

After we piled in the car, I felt kinda sorry for Bill watching him stand in the driveway with his mama, hugging her bony shoulders and whispering in her ear, his face not looking like Bills at all. Then I watched him walk down the driveway toward us, wiping his eyes with his handkerchief and I felt like I wanted to cry too. But as he got up to the car, I saw the real Bill again and heard him too, when he stuck his head in the side window and yelled, "I hope you girls remembered to pee, cause I'm telling you right now, once we pull out of here, were not stopping"

The Wheelchair

We took Jannie Mae to the fair in a wheelchair yesterday but it was no fun. In fact, it was awful. It rained hard, after we got there, just like it always does at the fair. I can't understand why they just don't change it to another month. April would be perfect, cause round here, September is too hot, the rain only brings out more mosquitoes and the air hangs sticky all over you, even if you're goin' fast on the Scrambler.

After fussin' about it last week, Mama made up her mind and told us, "Were gonna take Jannie Mae to the fair and that's that, so ya'll keep your big mouths shut. Now, I know there's bound to be somebody in this neighborhood who can loan us a wheelchair." It was embarrassing having Mama borrow stuff from people who lived around us, when you know they was always wishing we would move.

Jannie Mae has been doing ok since her bicycle accident back in May, although it really wasn't her bicycle. She borrowed it from Dianne Burpo and took off down Arkansas Road. A rich girl driving a Jeep way too fast hit Jannie Mae and the part of her brain that affects her balance got bruised real bad when she hit the road. She was in a coma for a week. I'm really glad they let her in St. Francis' Hospital, even though we are Southern Baptists, cause Mama said those sweet nuns lighting all them candles is what saved her. Mama and Bill have to drive Jannie Mae to Shreveport once a month now to a special doctor who takes pictures of her head and is helping her get her balance back so she can walk again.

I really didn't think Jannie Mae needed to go the fair. After all, she sits propped up in bed all day surrounded by pillows, so she won't topple over. She gets to watch TV, color and play Elvis records on the hi-fi. She got two new Barbie dolls in the hospital, and even got to drop out of the third grade.

It took one and a half hours to get Jannie Mae from her bed, into the car and then from the parking lot to the midway and the fair was only two miles from our house. Mama and me and Cathy Lee had to push that big old ugly wooden wheelchair, which wasn't easy, as Jannie Mae is a little chunky and added to that was the three pillows to help her sit up straight. Plus we had to put Sharon Rose in her lap as she's only four and couldn't really help push.

Mama found a man selling those cute little kewpie dolls with the feather dresses on the long sticks to tie on Jannie Mae's wheelchair. That only made it worse, cause after that, it looked like everybody was staring at us and feeling real sorry. I kept scrunching down behind the wheelchair, hoping and praying I would not see anyone from my fifth grade class, until Mama popped me upside the head, yelling out, "You keep hiding like that, Linda Rae and I'll give you something to really hide from, girl!"

Things were going okay, I guess, although Cathy Lee and I was real bored. Jannie Mae was getting excited about picking up them little yellow plastic ducks with the numbers on their bottoms. She won her a pair of straw Chinese handcuffs which she got stuck on her fingers. Mama made us cheer when Jannie Mae tried to knock down wooden milk bottles and throw darts at little balloons, which was half deflated by the heat. Jannie Mae was starting to look real pitiful.

We stopped in the building that had the farm animals but it stunk bad in there. When Jannie Mae tried to bend over to pet the baby goats, it made her dizzy and Mama real worried. Then we pushed her into the Home Building where we spent too much time looking at fudge, pies and cakes, none of which we could eat. It got hot in there and we was so hungry, we begged Mama to please let us go back outside on the midway.

Just when we was walking around looking for other exciting things that Jannie Mae could do, it started raining and I mean raining real hard. While Mama was getting out her drizzle bonnet, me and Cathy Lee ran and pushed the wheelchair under an open tent where they sold food. We found a table to sit at and Mama bought us corn dogs and french fries in paper cones, which was the highlight of my day. We had root beer, not in frosted glass mugs like I love, but it was still good. It just kept raining and raining and Mama warned us, "You girls better eat slow so we don't have to give up our table under here." Twenty-five minutes later, as Mama finished her third cigarette, the rain finally stopped.

We was surprised at how much mud was in the midway from all that rain. Jannie Mae was starting to feel a lot heavier after two corn dogs and all them french fries. Those big wheels was making deep ruts in the mud and that's how we got stuck. We could tell while rocking that wheelchair back and forth, and side to side, that that mud was not gonna let go of those wheels.

These two guys with great big arms who worked at the fair saw us and I guess they felt really bad cause they came over and tried to pull the wheelchair out of the mud. They couldn't budge it either, so one of them had to pick up Jannie Mae, while the other one finally got the wheelchair loose. Mama decided it was time to leave the fair then.

So here we was parading down the midway, the first man carrying Jannie Mae, the second man carrying the muddy wheelchair, with the little kewpie doll looking down on us all. Next was Mama carrying Sharon Rose, kicking and crying real loud cause she didn't want to leave all the fun. Then came Cathy Lee carrying them wet heavy pillows, and finally me grumbling under my breath, so Mama wouldn't hear me, "Five doggone hours at the fair and I didn't even get to ride the Tilt-a-Whirl."

Observing Arilla

The day after the insurance check came for Jannie Mae's accident, Bill made a down payment on a brand new Studebaker Lark and bought Mama a silver service tea set, well, silver-plated, that is. And Arilla started coming to our house three days a week. She helps Mama take care of Jannie Mae who can walk a little bit on her own now, but still wobbles and kinda looks like a drunk staggering around. Arilla is big and strong, so she's good at lifting Jannie Mae out of her bed and carrying her around the house. She also helps Mama with the ironing and cooking. I love Arilla's fried chicken and hot biscuits but don't talk much about that around Mama, so as not to hurt her feelings. We can't call Arilla our colored maid cause Mama says, "These damn nosy neighbors will gossip about us even more and call us uppity, which ya'll better never forget, we are not."

Linda Rae Johnson

Arilla is her honest to goodness real name but I don't know her last name. I can't imagine any mama giving a daughter she really loves a pitiful name like Arilla. Me and my sister, Cathy Lee, sometimes call her Arilla the Gorilla, but not to her face, cause Mama would slap ours hard if she heard that.

Arilla is the exact same color of Hershey's chocolate syrup and shiny like it too, cause she's always sweating, even if there's a cool rain falling outside. She is fat, and I mean every part of her is fat. She has a big round head and always wears the same faded blue checkered scarf tied around it. Arilla has two buck teeth sticking straight out in front of her mouth and I'm pretty sure they're the only teeth she's got. She don't seem embarrassed bout em' cause she's always smiling. Her shoes are faded black flats with the heels runned way down and crooked. They look real big on her feet, which are already huge anyway. Them shoes looks like she's been wearing em all her life. She always

48

wears faded dresses too, big ones, I guess around size forty-four, with them skinny little belts to match, but her huge belly always makes the belts curl inside out. She don't wear one piece of jewelry, not even a bangle bracelet and never wears makeup, or even red lipstick like Mama, although Arilla is so ugly, I don't think it would help much.

Arilla loves to listen to gospel music on the little transistor radio that Mama lets her keep on the end of the ironing board. She can sing pretty good, too, but not as good as she can iron or fry chicken. I once asked Arilla why she was always so happy, and she said, "Cause I is filled up with my Jesus and I is bound for the Kingdom."

Arilla looks a lot older than Mama but she couldn't be cause she has five young children, three girls and two boys. The girls are about our age so Mama gives Arilla our clothes when they get too dirty and ragged for us to wear anymore. Arilla always seems happy with whatever Mama gives her, even chicken necks and gizzards, which is just fine by me, cause that's two parts of the chicken I don't want nothing to do with.

Mama drives out in the country around nine and picks up Arilla and takes her home about three o'clock. Sometimes Mama takes her by the bread store, so Arilla can buy old half-moldy bread and stale crackers and cereal in bags that are all taped up cause they busted open.

One day Mama asked me if I wanted to ride with her to take Arilla home. There won't nothing else to do, so I said yeah. We drove outside of town on Devione Highway for about twenty minutes and then turned down a long dirt road, where there were little shacks lined up one after the other on both sides. Behind the shacks were big cotton fields and lots of colored people bent over picking cotton and dragging long dirty bags behind em. I couldn't believe in them cotton fields in the hot sun, there won't one shade tree, no lemonade stand and no ice cream truck. Some of the real old colored people were sittin out on their front porches, fanning themselves, trying to keep cool in the all that mugginess hanging around.

We drove up in front of Arilla's shack and I was surprised how many kids I saw out in the little dusty yard. As she got out of the car, they grinned and ran and wrapped themselves all around her body, the little ones hugging her legs. One girl with dirty feet and a broken comb stuck in her hair was wearing a dress that a long time ago used to be mine, when it blossomed bright yellow and orange flowers.

I looked for just a second into the front door of Arilla's house, but it was so dark in there I couldn't see nothing. You couldn't really call that shack a house, it was so old and worn, it looked like a little breeze, if there was ever one out that way, could've knocked it over in a second.

I got a sick feeling down in the pit of my belly and no words would come out so I just smiled and waved goodbye to Arilla and all those dirty little children. As we drove off in Bill's new Studebaker with the fresh smelling seats and eased out onto Devione Highway, I thought something about Arilla just didn't seem fair. Later in the evening, my head was filled up with a picture of her and her children eating chicken necks and stale bread for supper.

I know now that Arilla don't iron her little girls' dresses all nice and starchy like mine and don't feed em hot biscuits loaded down with butter and honey. I feel sad for her children, the cotton pickers and all those tired old colored people, but most of all I feel sad for Arilla and I swear to myself I will never again call her Arilla the Gorilla.

Two Dimwit Cousins

About a hundred miles south of West Monroe is the Louisiana State Hospital for the Criminally Insane. Me and my sisters call it "The Loony Bin." It's in Pineville which is also where Aunt Rosie, her husband, J. Davis and my two dimwit cousins, Jack Ray and Randy live. We go there once a year, for three days during Labor Day Holiday to have a picnic, all eleven of us. That's countin' their ugly Chihuahua with the bugged out eyes, Sweet Lilly, a stupid name for a stupid dog. Bill always says, "I'd love to stomp that dog's ass right in the ground" I think he really means it, but he'd never do that cause Sweet Lilly is almost like the baby girl that Rosie never had. Rosie, whose real name is Rosaline, is Bill's younger sister. She is ugly and mean just like my grandma, Ida. When Rosie ain't yelling at Jack Ray and Randy, she's griping to J. Davis about such things as needing a new icebox, the high price of slab bacon at the Be-Lo Market or her frizzy permanent wave. Mama says, "It's a good thing they live in Pineville, cause that woman is one pecan headin for a crack-up."

I can't understand how Rosie got a husband like J. Davis Miller. He's got to be the cutest man in Pineville with great big tanned arms, green eyes and wavy blonde hair that makes curls around the back of his neck when he'sweatin. He is from San Antonio, Texas and was named after Jefferson Davis who was president of the south during the Civil War. J. Davis owns a Texaco station where he fixes cars and pumps gas. He's just as funny as he is cute, tells the greatest Little Moron jokes I ever heard. My favorite is "Why did the Little Moron tiptoe past the medicine cabinet? He didn't wanna wake the sleeping pills." I love it when he takes me and my sisters for a ride in his tow truck with the flashing lights turned on. J. Davis can talk out of one side of his mouth while his teeth are clamped down on a Winston on the other side.

Jack Ray and Randy are 14 and 12. They're mean like their Mama but cute like their daddy. They both got his green eyes and that wavy blonde hair. Jack Ray keeps a little black comb in the back pocket of his blue jeans and I love to watch him pull out that comb and move it thru his hair. Randy is cute,too until he smiles. That's cause Jack Ray kicked out his two front teeth this summer while they was wrestling on the living room floor. When Rosie ain't looking, they're always giving us knuckle sandwiches, pulling the barrettes out of our hair or holding us down on the floor and pootin' on our heads. Once when we went fishing I saw Randy pick up a little baby alligator by the tail and hurl it thru the air.

Jack Ray and Randy are always getting in trouble. At our picnic last year, they stuck a cherry bomb in a watermelon and blew it up. Last summer they set their back yard on fire smoking monkey cigars from their catalpa tree. They even started up J. Davis' Chevy one night and drove it around the block. Rosie is always slapping em and lots of times I've seen J. Davis pulling off his belt threatening to give em a whipping.

How could two boys be so mean and so stupid,too? I heard J. Davis tell Mama that Randy had to take arithmetic over again in summer school and Jack Ray has to repeat 7th grade this year. I caught a glimpse of Jack Ray's school papers on their messy bedroom floor full of red marks and F's. Well, what do you expect? The only thing they read is Superman funny books.

While we were in Pineville, we had to make our own fun, which wasn't easy. On Saturday afternoon all us kids walked the three miles out to J. Davis's Texaco. We got to eat peanuts and drink Coca-Colas for free. We sat outside on a broken down picnic table behind the station and had a contest to see who could burp the most times. I hate to see Cathy Lee win at anything, but I was sure glad she whipped Jack Ray and Randy, burping twelve times in a row.

On Saturday night we all went to this little amusement park and got to ride all six of the rides there, except for the merry-go-round which Jack Ray said only a sissy would be caught dead on. We got excited about riding the ferris wheel and when Jack Ray climbed into the seat next to me, my heart started beating real fast. I was grinning just wishing my friend, Lettie Grantham, could've seen me sitting next to a cute boy, even if he was my dimwit cousin. It felt good knowing that if I got scared, Jack Ray would be right there next to me. Once the Ferris wheel started moving, I loved the way the warm wind felt hitting my face and looking out on the night lights of Pineville and the loony bin. Then our cart stopped right at the very top so some more kids could get on and I started getting scared and whining a little bit. Jack Ray called me a wimp and then that idiot started rocking the cart back and forth, howling and laughing. I was so scared, I started screaming loud enough for all of Pineville to hear me. Jack Ray then tried to stand up in the cart and I knew I was only seconds away from plunging to my death, my body splattering all over that amusement park. I could hear Rosie down below squealing like a little pig and J. Davis hollering up at Jack Ray "Boy, you better sit your ass down right now!!!" Then the Ferris wheel started movin again and when we got back down to the ground, I jumped out of that cart and ran crying to Mama, trembling with the truth that Jack Ray had almost killed me. And Rosie, well she almost killed Jack Ray, kept hitting him upside the head with her fat pocketbook yelling, "That's it, you little hellion, You're grounded for a week." I stopped sniffling then and started grinning.

On Monday afternoon when it was time to head back to West Monroe, I didn't mind huggin J. Davis goodbye but just as I gave Jack Ray a hug, he snuck in one last hard knuckle sandwich when no one was looking. I almost showed my bruised arm to Rosie. Then I thought how sorry I felt for Jack Ray repeating 7th grade all over again and Randy with his snaggle tooth grin, both of them stuck in that lousy town with their whiny Mama and Sweet Lilly, livin a little too close to the Looney Bin.

Loathing Lettie

I wonder if it's possible to love someone and at the same time hate em, too? I asked Mama and she said "Linda Rae, if you hate someone, then that means you wish em dead and cursed to hell." I wouldn't want Lettie Grantham to die and if she did I wouldn't want her to end up in hell. Lettie is my friend. We sit together at lunch sneaking food off each other's plate so Mrs. Ballard won't see us. We talk a lot and share secrets when were walking home from school. Every summer Lettie brings me a souvenir gift when she goes on vacation. Last year she brought me a pencil box from Albuquerque, New Mexico with an Indian squaw wearing a blue necklace painted on it. I go over to Lettie's house a lot. She can't come to my house, though cause of my crazy stepfather Bill and his temper which everyone in West Monroe knows about.

If I could be one person in the world, besides Annette Funicello, it would be Lettie. First of all, she is rich. Her daddy owns a furniture store in West Monroe. Her Mama's in a sorority, plays bridge once a week and makes ceramic vases in their basement. She 's always having luncheons and fixes the cutest little sandwiches with the crusts cut off filled with pink cream cheese, olives and deviled ham.

The Granthams live in a big house way out on Arkansas Road. They had their carport torn down and a matching brick garage built right onto the side of the house which now looks as long as the lunch counter at Woolworths. They got a huge back yard all fenced in with lots of trees and a little barn for Lettie's pony, Dapple. Their house has a family room with two sofas, a fireplace and knotty pine walls. It has three bedrooms. Mr. and Mrs. Grantham have their own bathroom so they don't have to walk down the hallway in the middle of the night when they have to pee. Lettie is the only kid in her family, so she don't have to share her hi-fi or fight with anyone about what record to play next. Her room has pink flowered wallpaper and a four-piece matching bedroom set called French Provincial which includes a nightstand for her pink Princess phone. Lettie says her bedroom set was shipped all the way from Paris, France. The bed has a white lace canopy over it. Whenever I spend the night with Lettie and I'm laying there looking up at that canopy, I know how Josephine Boneparte must've felt.

Lettie is the prettiest and most popular girl in the fifth grade. Her eyes are the same blue as a robin's egg and her hair is Barbie blonde. It's naturally wavy so her Mama don't have to pin curl her hair every night. Lettie 's teeth are so perfect and white, she could be in a Pepsodent commercial. The boys in our fifth grade class love looking and grinning at Lettie. Even a few of the sixth grade boy's whistle at her and hang out at her locker every morning before the bell rings. Lettie wears a training bra, which Mama says shouldn't make me feel bad cause you really can't train em and in the end they're gonna go off in the direction they want to. Mostly south.

Lettie wears multi-colored crinolines under her dresses that look like a rainbow when she twirls around. She has shorts of every color all with flowered blouses, velvet hair bands and flip-flops to match. No matter how long Lettie plays outside, her clothes never wrinkle, get sweat stains or dirt on em. She has a 14-karat gold bracelet with eight charms on it. One of the charms is a silver record with a shiny red jewel right in the middle of it Sometimes I ask her "Lettie, can I wear your charm bracelet, please?" And she always hollers back, "No, Lnda Rae!! I told you already that's a real ruby.

Deep down inside me, I feel there is something about Lettie that just don't seem fair. Like when it's hot and were walking home from school and my hair gets all sweaty and sticking to my head and her hair still keeps them pretty blonde waves. Lke the way she grins right back at the boys who don't seem to mind that she is kinda dumb. Lettie don't even know who Helen Keller or Nikita Kruschev is. And she takes a long time to diagram a five-word sentence.

Me and my three sisters share the same room with two double beds and the only reason our bedroom set matches is cause Mama spent a whole Saturday afternoon painting it blue. I do have a charm bracelet from G.C. Murphy's that came with one charm, a stupid looking flower. My arm turns green every time I wear it. Mama never cuts the crust off our sandwiches cause she says it's just too wasteful. The room we watch TV in has one sofa, gray and lumpy, a coffee table and Bill's recliner which we are not allowed to jump on, climb on, sit on or lean up against.

I think Mama understands sometimes how I feel about Lettie. She says there are good qualities and beauty in me that Lettie could never have like not telling fibs. "Honey, there is no way that bedroom set came from France and what fool parent is gonna buy an eleven year old a real ruby."

Mama's always right. People tell me all the time I look just like Darla on *The Little Rascals*. I make good grades in school, too. Mrs. Ballard gave me an A+ last month on my geography report "Switzerland, Land of the Alps" Everyone howls and laughs when I make up knock-knock jokes. And no one can beat me at Chinese Checkers. Not even Lettie.

Last Sunday afternoon it was pouring down rain so hard we couldn't go outside to play. Me and Cathy Lee was having a Jacks championship on our bedroom floor. Mama was cutting out paper dolls with Jannie Mae and Sharon Rose. Bill wadn't yelling - that's cause he was taking a nap in his recliner. Lettie called me on the phone and wanted to know if I could come over to her house. I told her, "No, Lettie I 'm up to my eightsies on pigs in the pens and me and Cathy Lee are running neck and neck for the championship. I'll call you back later." I couldn't wait to get back to the game. But I kept thinking about Lettie in that big pink bedroom, listening to records on her hi-fi all by herself, probably wishing she had someone to play jacks or cut out paper dolls with. I felt kinda sorry for Lettie. I messed up on my tensies but Cathy Lee made it through hers. She jumped up laughing, thumped me upside the head and reminded me, "Now, Miss Loser, you gotta wash the dishes all week."

"Shut up, Cathy Lee you make me sick." But it really didn't matter. I was glad it was all over. I couldn't wait to get over to Lettie's house. And runnin' as fast as I could, I kept thinkin "Maybe...this is the day I'll finally get to wear that solid gold charm bracelet."

Uncovering Santa

I'm glad Christmas is over and 1958 is almost here. Mama says me and my sisters can stay up till midnight on New Years Eve, light sparklers, drink ginger ale and eat all the peanut butter cookies we want. This year Christmas changed for me and it will never be the same again. I knew I had to face the truth, which Clyde Poche, the meanest and the fattest boy in my neighborhood had been telling me all year long. "Linda Rae, you dimwit, there's no such thing as Santa Claus. It's all a big lie." I thought he was making it up as Clyde's Mama and Daddy are real strict Catholics, so they spend all their Christmas holiday lighting candles, saying their Hail Marys and going to Mass which Clyde can't even understand cause he don't speak Latin.

Finding out the truth about Santa Claus won't really my fault. Like everything bad that happens to me, it all started with my sister, Cathy Lee.

Three weeks ago we're out on the carport playing basketball, seeing who could score ten points first. I was winning and kinda rubbing it in, which made Cathy Lee real mad and she started stomping and screaming, and quit the game, like losers always do. She then threw the basketball so hard at me, it bounced off the carport floor and landed up in the rafters. Bill had nailed some boards across the rafters for storing boxes. Well, the only way I could get to that ball was using Bill's tall ladder, which didn't bother me one bit as I ain't scared of high places.

I couldn't believe my eyes, way up in those rafters hidden behind the boxes, was our Christmas toys, most everything we wanted and had been talking about for months. My Howdy Doody record player, a green autograph poodle and a Heckel and Jeckel lunch box for Cathy Lee. There was Jannie Mae's Annie Oakley outfit with a white holster and two silver cap guns and a big stuffed bunny with floppy pink ears for my little sister, Sharon Rose.

Plus all kinds of games for us, Parcheesi, Chinese Checkers and even Monopoly. I got this sick feeling like I was gonna throw up cause I knew at that very moment big fat Clyde was telling the turth. There was no such thing as Santa Claus. There it was, our Christmas wishes, picked out and paid for by Bill and Mama, all ready to put under the tree and fool us on Christmas morning. I knew I had to keep the secret to myself cause if Cathy Lee, the biggest tattletale in the world, found out I saw all them toys, she would run blabbing to Mama and Bill, which would get me a whipping and into a whole lot of trouble.

The next day Mama took us to Sears-Roebuck in Monroe and I had to sit there on Santa's lap and grin at him, even though I could see the glue holding that phony beard on his face and smell his bologna and onion breath. Faking that big Ho-Ho-Ho and asking me what I wanted him to bring me, like he could really care. Telling me the biggest lie of all, "Linda Rae, if you're a good little girl, I'll bring you all the toys you want." Then I had to force myself to give him a hug while his stupid elf took a picture of us. I couldn't figure out who was faking the worse, me or him.

Last Saturday when Mama took us to the Christmas parade in Monroe, I could really see what a big lie Santa Claus was. The Santa sitting on top of that fire truck waving and throwing candy at all the kids did not look one bit like the Santa at Sears-Roebuck. At least his beard and his stomach looked real but how could I have been so stupid?

As Christmas got closer, I tried not to get mad thinking about Santa Claus. It did make me happy seeing my sisters getting excited about Christmas, especially Sharon Rose whose only four. And we did have fun helping Bill decorate the tree, until he blew up cause Jannie Mae picked up a bunch of icicles he had laid out one by one on the back of a chair and threw them on the tree. "Phyllis, get these damn brats out of here right now so I can finish this tree" But that night after it was all decorated, Mama let us lay on the living room in our pajamas, staring at the tree and all those beautiful colored lights glowing and twinkling in the dark and singing our favorite Christmas songs. Mine is *Rocking Around the Christmas Tree* by Brenda Lee.

We got a whole lot of Christmas cards and Mama taped them up around the living room door. She hung our stockings on the doorknobs ause we don't' have a fireplace. We had big stockings with our names written in silver glitter. Since I am the oldest and don't get on Mama's nerves like my sisters do, I got to help her in the kitchen on Christmas Eve. She let me put the marshmallows on the sweet potatoes and get the ham ready for the oven, covering it with pineapple, cloves and maraschino cherries.

On Christmas morning Sharon Rose woke us up at 6 o'clock and we hurried into the living room to have a look at what I knew was already gonna be there. But seeing all them toys under the tree and hearing my sisters squealing and hollering got me all excited. I couldn't help but jump up and down when I saw my Howdy Doody record player. Plus lots of other gifts all wrapped up in pretty paper and shiny bows. My stocking was filled fat with candy canes, tangerines, chocolates wrapped in silver and gold and my favorite card games, Old Maid and Crazy Eights.

Later that evening, I felt so lucky laying across my bed, listening to Elvis singing *Heartbreak Hotel* on my new record player, my belly filled up with ham biscuits and sweet potatoes. And I couldn't help grinning thinking about Clyde Poche, putting on his new scratchy white shirt and stupid looking bow tie, getting ready for Mass...again.

Rosemary and Theodore

I wish that Mama and Bill had never bought Jannie Mae those two little rabbits, Rosemary and Theodore, last June for her birthday. It only made more problems for us, as Bill was already known around the neighborhood as a madman. Now a dog killer, too. He despises dogs, and that was long before Rosemary and Theodore got here. What he does loves most in the world, better then me or my three sisters, is his yard and all his flowers and them miniature fruit trees, especially the figs. Before he bought the pistol, the dogs made him scream and cuss in the mornings, when he would discover dog poops all around his little trees or his flowers trampled on by big unknown paws.

Last spring, when Bill built a new carport and had finally spread out the wet cement just to his liking, me and Cathy Lee saw two dogs from Jersey Avenue track thru it, leaving a big mess behind.

We was really scared and he blew up so bad that Mama warned all four of us, "Ya'll get out of his way and you stay out of his way. In fact, go on, get to your room right now and don't you dare come out till I tell you to." And we didn't. It wasn't until supper when Mama put a big plate of pork chops and stewed tomatoes in front of Bill, that he smiled and rubbed her back and me and my sisters knew we could be real again.

I had no idea that Rosemary and Theodore would multiply like they did and we'd end up with all them rabbits, but by March we had fifty-two of em. Bill kept building more pens and then he got this smart idea to sell some at Easter. He did sell eighteen babies for $2 each, but when April was gone, we still had lots of rabbits and more of a reason for the dogs to come around in the middle of the night. They'd be out there and start whining and scratching at the pens and yelping at each other to see who could get to a rabbit first.

I remember the first time I heard the pistol go off. It sounded so loud, like it was the end of the world, the way church people talk about it, you know, in the book of Revelations. After a couple of weeks, though, we got used to the sound. At least we would get a warning, Bill jerking the nightstand drawer open and yelling, "Those son of a bitching dogs, I'm gonna kill every sorry ass one of em." Then he would throw open the window screen and start firing the pistol into the black midnight of our backyard.

The next morning would always be the scariest. It'd be real early and I'd sneak out of my bed and peek through the curtains to see if there were any maimed or worse yet, dead, stiff dogs piled up in our backyard. Sometimes, standing at the window, with my eyes shut tight, I'd get that feeling right before you throw up that I'd look out and see Happy, the little collie, that belonged to my best friend, Billie Stell.

Linda Rae Johnson

Word got around the neighborhood and at my school that Bill was killing dogs in our backyard. Actually, he only killed one, a skinny, yellow, mangy dog that looked like it never had a home or was loved by anyone, especially from my school, so I didn't feel too bad.

It's July now and I'm glad school's out. Jannie Mae gets sad sometimes cause she misses Rosemary and Theodore. We got rid of the rabbits last month and Bill got rid of the pistol. The last dog he shot at was a boxer that belonged to Clint Russell's daddy, a Louisiana state trooper. The bullet only grazed Tinka's leg, but Sergeant Russell was plenty mad. He came banging on our front door and when Bill opened it, fists started flying, they lost their balance, fell back onto the living room floor, rolling around and grunting, and then Bill got punched out. I ran to my room, slammed the door, jumped on my bed, buried my head deep in my pillow and laughed and laughed. Maybe it will be a good summer after all.

Not Far From Dallas

I feel sorry for Mama sometimes, especially when Bill is yelling at her. He's the kind of devil that kisses her neck and holds her tight one minute and then knocks a plate of fried okra out of her hand the next, just because its shade of brown ain't quite to his liking. If you take a real close look at Bill when he's grinning his fake horsy smile, you can see a lot of meanness right behind his eyes.

Oh, he does takes good care of us, Mama and me and my three sisters. Me and Cathy Lee are taking tap and paton every Wednesday afternoon at Lisa Lavender's Dance Studio. At my birthday party last year, Bill hired a clown to do magic tricks with a pony to take my friends for a ride around the back yard. But when the party was over and everyone was gone, Bill started his ranting and raving when he stepped in pony poop. "That damn sorry ass clown and his son of a bitching pony, leaving here and not even cleaning up this crap." It won't the clown's fault. It won't the pony's fault either. But Bill's got to have something or somebody to yell at when things ain't going his way, which, believe me, is most of the day and sometimes right on into the evening.

This summer I am well on my way to becoming a famous actress. I tried out and got the part of Melinda Loomis in a play called *Inherit the Wind* opening next Friday night at the Ouachita Little Theater in Monroe. I don't have too many lines, except in one court scene, although at the beginning of the play, I get to dance across the stage with an old stuffed monkey all by myself. Mama and I go to rehearsals three nights a week, which is fun cause I love it when it's just me and Mama. She sits out in the theater a couple of rows behind the director, whispering with the other mamas and just grinning at me cause she's so proud.

Last night, after me and Mama left rehearsal, she said, "Linda Rae, honey, how would you like to stop off at the Hollywood for some Curly Q's and a root beer?" The Hollywood Café - it's a little ways outside of Monroe on Louisville Highway, a big square pink building, got no windows, but neon lights all around it. It looks like New Years Eve and inside it feels the same way, cool and sparkling with big round booths a whole family could fit in. Them soft Naugahyde seats got that smell just like new shoes. And best of all, the Hollywood has a big jukebox, filled with colored lights and probably 50 songs to pick from.

Everybody for miles around knows about the Hollywood and its famous Curly Q's. We hardly ever go there cause we live all the way in West Monroe and Mama says it's just too far to drive for a basket of fried potatoes. Mama's real sensible about things like that.

While we was sitting there in our booth waiting for the waitress, in the door all the way from Jersey Avenue, walked Mr. Dallas Freeman, our next door neighbor. Mama just grinned and wiggled her red fingernails at him. He walked over to our booth, dressed in a beige suit and wearing a baby blue bow tie with a handkerchief to match, looking like somebody who knew how to keep cool in summer. He said to me as he pinched my cheek and winked at Mama, "Well, hello there, Linda Rae! How's the little actress?" He smelled like Old Spice and his wavy brown hair was all combed and neat, glistening with Brylcream. His upper lip was glistening too, shaking a little bit and he took out his handkerchief and patted it dry. Then he slid into the booth next to Mama, reached in his pocket, pushed two quarters across the table and said, "Go on, Linda Rae and pick out a couple of your favorite songs on the jukebox."

Mr. Freeman is a nice man considering what he's got to live with. His wife stays in bed all the

80

time wearing the same ole nasty nightgown, smoking cigarettes, drinking Schlitz and peeing on the sheets. They got two girls, Netty Sue and Pauline and both of them are pretty pitiful. Netty Sue, who's thirteen, fell against, a wood stove when she was two and got her face and neck all burned up. Pauline is sixteen, never opens her mouth or washes her hair. She stays locked in her bedroom all day, reading yellow paperbacks. I guess that's why she needs them thick, ugly glasses. Pauline's almost as scary to look at as Netty Sue. Me and my sisters go over their house sometimes, but we can't hardly stand it, it stinks so bad. Their grandma comes twice a week - does the smelly laundry piled up in the hallway, cooks casseroles and mops up the ants crawling across the kitchen floor.

I felt so lucky standing at that jukebox, listening to Bobby Darin singing *Mack The Knife* and being real grown up picking my very own favorite songs, *I'm Sorry* by Brenda Lee, Ray Charles, *Hit the Road*

Jack and my favorite Elvis, *All Shook Up* and I still got two more songs to play.

I looked over at the booth. Mama and Mr. Freeman were talking low and smiling and I noticed when Mama threw her head back and laughed at him how pretty she looked, wearing her sleeveless, red shell and perfect matching lipstick. Her face turned all pink when Mr. Freeman started smelling her hair, it was probably the Prell.

Mama just loves Patsy Cline, cause so many people tell her she looks just like Patsy so I decided to play *Walking After Midnight* and *Crazy* just for her. Mr. Freeman then called out and waved me over to a big basket piled high with Curly Q's and a mug of ice cold root beer. Mama and Mr. Freeman had mugs too, filled with beer, and I liked the way the frost looked dripping down their mugs, making shiny little puddles on the table.

I couldn't stop laughing when Mr. Freeman pulled dimes out of his ears and told me and Mama jokes. He has a nice soft voice and didn't even yell at me when I spilt ketchup all over the table. When Patsy Cline started singing *Crazy*, Mama blew me a kiss across the booth. Mr. Freeman must love Patsy Cline too, cause he moved over closer to Mama, put his arm around her shoulder and whispered in her ear. Mama smiled, laid her head back on his arm, closed her eyes and started singing that pretty song right along with Patsy.

On the way home, after we left the Hollywood, Mama told me that we had a special secret between us about our new friend, Mr. Freeman. She said that Bill would blow his top if he found out about it, but I already knew that. Believe me, I ain't gonna say or do anything to make Bill mad. Besides I could eat Curly Q's and drink root beer every night of the week. I feel so close to Mama cause of our "Hollywood Secret". Mama says she's so happy about me being such a good little actress, she wants

me to try out for the next play called The Miracle Worker.

Going Home with Peanut

Peanut got here today and is gonna take us home. He drove straight thru from Highland Springs, Virginia to West Monroe, Louisiana and that ain't no fun in August with no air conditioner or sleep for twenty-one hours. I am thirteen and the oldest of my sisters so Mama says she can explain the truth to me and I will understand.

He is not really our Uncle Raymond or Peanut, which is his nickname and what we call him. He is and has always been our real daddy, even when Bill Fordyce convinced Mama of a new promised land in Louisiana filled with magnolias, a brick house, and a daddy for her four girls. I was six then, confused, but not stupid, cause I knew that Bill was not or could never be our real daddy. My three sisters was too little to figure it all out like me. But after all these years, Mama says my real daddy is gonna do right by us.

I remember the three times Peanut visited us here in West Monroe. He brought us M&Ms, big Fritoes and dark green sunglasses with white frames and little rhinestones. He took us to the drive-in to see Elvis in *Jailhouse Rock*, and let us sit on the hood of his car even though we was wearing pajamas and sponge rollers.

I don't really blame Mama for calling Peanut to get us out of West Monroe. I think she is just tired of crying and worrying about having enough money to pay the rent so we won't get kicked out, and buying enough groceries to last another week. Since Bill got taken away in May for cheating the insurance company he worked for, I'm getting plenty sick and tired of potted meat, saltines and Kool-aid.

Mama says I have to be strong and help my sisters get packed up. I hope there'll be room for all six of us in Peanut's blue Ford. There are some things we'll have to leave behind cause he only brought a small trailer. But I know that Mama will let me take my two Elvis scrapbooks and my pompoms. She will have to talk to Peanut, though, about taking our cat, Penny, who is so old, she only has four teeth but two brand new kittens born last Sunday in our underwear cause Cathy Lee forgot to shut the drawer.

I think I will like it in Highland Springs. Peanut says he has a house for us to move into with a washing machine and a clothesline out back. I smile when I think of that, no more scraping together dimes and dragging our dirty clothes six blocks down to Lena's Wash Tub. I wonder if Peanut will live with us in our new house and kiss on Mama like Bill used to do. He says our last name will be Hunt again, not Fordyce. That will be hard for me because I have to start junior high in a new school, in a new town, with a new name. Peanut says that my Aunt Dolly and Uncle Ed will

Linda Rae Johnson

be nearby, and five cousins to play with, three girls and two boys. I hope the boys are cute.

I'm trying not to cry thinking about leaving tomorrow but Peanut says that everything will be okay. He's gonna take us across a big bridge over the Mississippi River and we'll get to wind around mountains near a town called Chattanooga and that'll be fun. We get to sleep one night in a motel and order anything we want for breakfast. And Peanut says we can play his car radio as loud as we want all the way to Highland Springs, Virginia.

About the Author

Ms. Linda Johnson, who lives in Richmond, Virginia credits her first summer in 1997 at the Nimrod Writers Retreat in Bath County, Virginia where she wrote "Monopoly at Twelve," as the beginning of her *Ouachita Girl* series, now totaling twenty-one vignettes. In the time since, she has enjoyed reading and performing her stories throughout Virginia. Some of her Richmond appearances have included the Barksdale Theater, Artspace Gallery, Virginia Museum of Fine Arts and the Jefferson Hotel. Outside of Richmond, she has shared her stories at Windy River Winery in Beaverdam, Virginia, Roanoke's Mill Mountain Theater and the Homestead Resort. She has appeared three times at the Greenbrier Resort in West Virginia and did a one-night reading/performance in April at New York City's Pulse Ensemble Theater. She has been an interviewed guest on Richmond's WCVE Public

Radio's *Gallery*. Two of her stories have been published in the Allegheny/Bath County literary journal, *Lumina*.

For additional information check out Linda Rae's website at: ouachitagirl.com

To book a performance reading or purchase *Ouachita Girl* - Volume 1 on CD contact Linda Johnson at raewriter@aol.com

Printed in the United States
6941

9 781403 319630